Rethinking Libel, Defamation, and Press Accountability

Carson Holloway

Washington Fellow

The Claremont Institute's CENTER FOR THE AMERICAN WAY OF LIFE

Design: **David Reaboi**/Strategic Improvisation

Published in the United States by the Claremont Institute

RETHINKING LIBEL, DEFAMATION, AND PRESS ACCOUNTABILITY

In 1964, the Supreme Court imposed a new regime of press freedom on the country. Before *New York Times v. Sullivan*, all Americans, even those active in public life, could sue and recover damages from anyone, including journalists, who had libeled them. Under the traditional standards, the truth of a statement was a defense again a claim of libel. Accordingly, the press was free to publish even scathing criticism of politicians, provided that the criticism was truthful. But when journalists published falsehoods, whether willfully or carelessly, they opened themselves up to lawsuits from those whose reputations they had harmed.

New York Times v. Sullivan and subsequent cases, however, swept away these traditional standards and the wholesome legal restraint they had imposed on the power of the press. From now on, the Court announced, the press would be held to a different and much more lenient standard when it falsely maligned public figures. Public figures could sue successfully for libel only if they could demonstrate that their defamers had acted with "actual malice"—that is, that they had knowingly published a falsehood or had acted with reckless disregard for the truth. Unsurprisingly, this standard proved almost impossible to meet in practice, with the result that the press has become almost completely free to defame prominent Americans with legal impunity.

The consequences of *New York Times v. Sullivan* have been baleful for our nation. The ruling has undermined self-government by giving the press immense power over the public mind. Today, a partisan press routinely attempts to shape political outcomes by using defamation to make some people and some positions odious to the public. The more successful a leader on the Right becomes, the more likely that person is to be labeled a racist or a Nazi. Critics of America's foreign policy establishment are frequently accused—without evidence—of being "puppets" of foreign leaders or in the pay of foreign governments. These smears—retailed so freely today—would have required much more caution in pre-1964 America, when they might well have landed their purveyors in court, with a real chance of having to pay damages.

The *New York Times* doctrine has also undermined our nation's commitment to equality. It creates unjustifiable inequalities—between ordinary citizens and public figures (whose reputations are less protected), between journalists and all other professionals (who, unlike reporters, must face the consequences of their negligence), and between the press and public figures (most of whom have little power to resist a corporate media determined to assail their reputations). Finally, *New York Times v. Sullivan* runs counter to one of the basic aims of American government: to secure the natural rights of all. Reputation, as the American Founders teach us, is a right as fundamental and as precious, and as deserving of the government's protection, as life, liberty, and property.

Moreover, these grave evils by no means result from a necessary fidelity to the Constitution. On the contrary, they arise from constitutional infidelity. With its opinion in *New York Times v. Sullivan*, the Supreme Court of 1964 was not discovering and adhering to the original meaning of the First Amendment. It was, rather, departing from that meaning and imposing its own novel standards on our nation's First Amendment jurisprudence. The key elements of the *New York Times* doctrine—the distinction between public figures and all other Americans, and the burden on the former to demonstrate "actual malice" in order to prevail in a libel action—are not rooted in the original understanding of the First Amendment. The original understanding instead held that libel—false, defamatory publication—is outside the freedom of the press and not protected by that venerable principle. Accordingly, today's Supreme Court should, at the earliest suitable opportunity, reverse *New York Times v. Sullivan* and return our nation to its traditional, and more wholesome and reasonable, standards of libel.

NEW YORK TIMES V. SULLIVAN: A REVOLUTION IN LIBEL LAW

New York Times v. Sullivan arose in the context of the civil rights movement. In 1960, the Committee to Defend Martin Luther King and the Struggle for Freedom in the South took out a full-page political advertisement in the *New York Times*. Titled "Heed Their Rising Voices," the ad condemned Southern leaders who were resisting desegregation, and in particular criticized the public officials in Montgomery, Alabama, for trying to suppress civil rights protests. Contending that he had been defamed by the ad, L. B. Sullivan, one of Montgomery's elected city commissioners, sued the *New York Times*, as well as four black

Alabama clergymen who were signatories to the ad. The Alabama trial court ruled for Sullivan and awarded him $500,000 in damages, a verdict upheld by the Alabama Supreme Court. The Supreme Court of the United States, however, reversed this judgment, holding that Sullivan could not demonstrate that he had been defamed—even though "Heed Their Rising Voices" admittedly contained several false statements.

The problem with *New York Times v. Sullivan* is not the ruling it announced but the new doctrine it introduced into American constitutional law. The justices had good grounds for finding against Sullivan. There was reason to think that he and other official litigants were using Alabama libel law to silence criticism from Northern newspapers.[1] Moreover, "Heed Their Rising Voices" did not mention Sullivan by name or even identify the office he occupied. The ad was more of a general condemnation of Southern official intransigence and intimidation, so that Sullivan had to argue that he had been defamed by implication. His libel claim, then, was weak and did not deserve to prevail.

As Justice Clarence Thomas has observed, the Supreme Court could have rested its ruling on these considerations alone.[2] The justices instead took an important further step, which has distorted American politics ever since. Writing for a unanimous Court, Justice William Brennan used the *New York Times* ruling to revise the country's constitutional jurisprudence regarding libel and freedom of speech and of the press. The First Amendment, he wrote, requires that "public officials" who are suing for libel in relation to claims made about their "official conduct" have to be treated differently than all other litigants. To succeed, they must show not only that they were defamed by the publication of false allegations. They must also meet the high standard of demonstrating that the publisher of the defamatory material acted with "actual malice." That is, public officials must now prove the publisher acted either with knowledge that the allegations were false, or with a "reckless disregard" for whether those allegations were false or true.[3] Subsequent cases further developed this doctrine. Not only "public officials" but even "public figures," who, as such, fall into a broader and vaguer category, now have to demonstrate "actual malice" to prevail in a defamation case.[4]

New York Times v. Sullivan thus created a revolution in libel law, one that has done great harm to our politics. Prior to this ruling, public figures (like anyone else) could sue and recover damages from those who had libeled them. The truth of a claim was considered a defense against libel. Journalists were therefore free to publish even biting criticism of public figures, so long as the criticism was based on accurate information. Those who went beyond the truth, however, placed themselves in legal jeopardy. Thus the pre-*New York Times* libel standards provided for freedom of the press while at the same time placing in the hands of public figures a legal check on the abuses of press freedom—a check that worked both to protect the reputations of individuals and to promote the truthfulness of public discourse.

The *New York Times* doctrine, however, effectively put an end to this wholesome legal check on the power of the press. Truth remains a defense against a charge of libel. For public figures, however, defamatory untruths are no longer sufficient to establish libel. To bring a successful libel action, public figures must now demonstrate both that the published material was defamatory and false, and that it was published with "actual malice"—that is, again, with knowledge of its falsehood or reckless disregard for its truth or falsehood.

Obviously, it is much easier to demonstrate that a claim is false and defamatory than to demonstrate anything about the state of mind of the person who made the claim. In practice, it is nearly impossible to prove actual malice, and the standard simply invites journalists to be careless, or to feign carelessness, about the truth, since mere carelessness does not rise to the level of actual malice. As David A. Logan observes, the *New York Times* standard creates a "perverse incentive" for journalistic institutions to lower their editorial standards, since, to recover damages, "the plaintiff must prove that the defendant knew the statement was false or was subjectively certain of its falsity." In these legal circumstances, "publishing without verification is the safest legal route, as an attempt to verify that turns up contrary information before publication can constitute reckless disregard for the truth and support liability. As a result, publishers are incentivized to do little or no fact-checking, confident that the more slipshod their investigation, the less likely they are to be guilty of 'actual malice.'"[5] The public figure's difficulty in prevailing is reflected in the small and diminishing number of cases brought against the media in the post-*New York Times v. Sullivan* era.[6] Journalists today thus have no serious legal obligation to publish only the truth. The *New York Times* standard has consequently made much American journalism a threat to the reputations of blameless public figures and given the press an enormous and destructive power over the public discourse and the public mind.

Several examples drawn from our history illustrate the magnitude of the change. In the early nineteenth century, the *New York American* published a story falsely claiming that the New York state attorney general had drunkenly presided over the legislature. When the attorney general sued, the editors attempted a defense that anticipated the later *New York Times* standard, holding that they could not be found liable if they had not known the story was false. The trial judge, however, rejected this standard and permitted the jury to award damages—an outcome that was affirmed on appeal.[7]

As the nineteenth century drew to a close, substantially the same libel standard was upheld by William Howard Taft, future president of the United States and chief justice of the Supreme Court, then serving as a judge of the United States Court of Appeals for the Sixth Circuit. In the case in question, Theodore Hallam, a failed congressional candidate, sued the *Cincinnati Post* for publishing an article falsely claiming that Hallam had been bribed to support another candidate. Hallam won his case, and when the Post Publishing Company appealed, Taft affirmed the verdict—and rejected the company's argument that the article, though false, should not be actionable if published in good faith.[8]

This standard was still being applied in the middle of the twentieth century. In 1941, prior to America's entry into the Second World War, journalist John O'Donnell published an article claiming that the Roosevelt administration was secretly shipping war supplies to Great Britain. President Roosevelt promptly condemned the story as a "deliberate lie." Shortly thereafter, the pro-Roosevelt *Philadelphia Record* published an editorial labeling O'Donnell as an open "Naziphile"—a supporter of "most of Hitler's aims," including the "liquidation of Jews." O'Donnell sued for libel and won. On appeal, the *Record* contended that the judgment violated its constitutional right to freedom of the press and that its liability should have been judged on whether it had published the editorial "solely for the purpose of causing harm to the plaintiff." In 1947, the appeals court rejected this argument, holding instead that "want of reasonable care and diligence to ascertain the truth, before giving currency to an untrue publication," properly exposes a publisher to a libel claim.[9]

In all these cases, public figures used libel law to protect their reputations and to hold the press accountable for spreading defamatory misinformation. In none of the cases was it possible for the publishers to defend themselves merely by claiming that they had not deliberately lied or acted with a reckless disregard for the truth. Rather, the standards followed by the courts presupposed that libel was not protected by freedom of the press, and that libel had occurred—and was actionable—even when the publisher had propagated falsehood through carelessness or negligence. Put another way, the standards then prevailing assumed that the publisher had a duty to exercise some diligence in ascertaining the truth before publishing.

The nation that lived under these reasonable and decent limitations nevertheless understood itself to be committed to the freedom of the press. In fact, that nation sought to support a press that was both free and restrained by a duty to tell the truth, instead of one that was licentious, abusive, and dishonestly inflammatory. Soon, however, those salutary standards were to be swept away by the Supreme Court's ruling in *New York Times v. Sullivan*, thus laying the foundations for the corrosive press culture from which America suffers today.

A most striking example of the change wrought by the *New York Times* ruling is provided by the experience of Washington state legislator John Goldmark. Goldmark was defeated for reelection in 1961 after a number of critics had publicly condemned him as a communist. He then brought a libel suit against several individuals and organizations, including a newspaper, that had been responsible for promoting these damaging claims. Goldmark prevailed: in early 1964, the jury in his case awarded him $40,000 in damages. Nevertheless, while post-trial motions were still pending in his case, the Supreme Court announced its ruling in *New York Times v. Sullivan*. Accordingly, Goldmark's trial judge, while admitting that the evidence showed the man was not a communist, nevertheless set aside the jury's verdict, since nothing in the record showed that Goldmark's libelers had known their claims were false or had acted with reckless disregard for the truth.[10]

The *New York Times* case thus ushered in a new era in American libel law in which public figures often cannot succeed in suing for libel even when they have been the victims of press defamation—an era, that is, in which there is no effective legal check by which to hold the press accountable for failing to publish the truth. In 1983, for example, *Time* magazine published a story claiming that, while serving as Israel's defense minister, Ariel Sharon encouraged the massacre of hundreds of Palestinians by a Lebanese Christian militia. When Sharon sued in the courts of the United States, the jury found that *Time's* story was false and defamatory; but they ruled for *Time* nonetheless, since there was no evidence that the magazine had acted with actual malice.[11]

In 2012, NBC News selectively edited the audio of the 911 call that George Zimmerman made prior to fatally shooting Trayvon Martin. The edit made it appear that Zimmerman was preoccupied with the fact that Martin was black, when in fact he had mentioned Martin's race in response to questioning by the emergency dispatcher. Zimmerman sued NBC for defamation and lost. Even though NBC apologized and admitted that the edit was an error, the judge in the case found that Zimmerman had no right to damages, since he was a public figure and had not proved that NBC had acted with malice.[12]

Most recently, former Republican vice presidential candidate Sarah Palin brought a defamation suit against the *New York Times* for an editorial falsely linking Palin's political rhetoric to a 2011 mass shooting in Arizona. The *Times* admitted that its claim was erroneous. Nevertheless, Palin's suit failed because she was a public figure and could not show actual malice on the part of the *Times*.[13]

These cases demonstrate the important change in our legal and political culture caused by *New York Times v. Sullivan*. Prior to this ruling, public figures possessed in American libel standards a legal tool by which to vindicate their reputations and hold journalists to account for publishing defamatory falsehoods. Since *New York Times v. Sullivan*, however, the wholesome restraint imposed on the press by the law of libel has practically vanished. Now, even those public figures who have admittedly been victimized by falsehood cannot sue successfully, since it is so hard to prove the recklessness and deliberate mendacity that characterize actual malice.

HOW THE *NEW YORK TIMES* DOCTRINE UNDERMINES DEMOCRACY AND EQUALITY

Our circumstances tend to blind us to the tremendous damage the *New York Times* ruling has done to our nation. Accustomed to and formed by the unrestrained public culture that the "actual malice" standard has spawned, many Americans have come to believe that freedom includes an unlimited license to abuse the nation's elected leaders and other public figures at will. For such Americans, a reversal of *New York Times v. Sullivan* appears as a threat to democracy itself. This view is entirely incorrect. In truth, the *New York Times* doctrine undermines democracy by eroding our country's capacity for genuine self-government and its commitment to equality.

Justice Brennan's opinion in *New York Times v. Sullivan* defended the "actual malice" standard as necessary to preserving the vigorous public discussion on which successful self-government depends. The principle he chose to embed in American law, however, is in fact hostile to the end he was trying to achieve. Successful self-government depends on a public discourse that is not only vigorous but also accurate and enlightening. Under the "actual malice" standard, the media have little incentive to sustain such a discourse, for they effectively have no legal obligation to tell the truth about public figures. The result is a public discourse that diminishes the quality of democratic representation and undermines the quality of democratic deliberation.

The system of representative self-government does not necessarily result in good and enlightened government. Under such a system, the quality of government will necessarily depend on the quality of the people elected to public office. The flourishing of our republic requires that those elected to positions of public responsibility are, to the extent possible, people of ability and integrity. Human conditions are such that there is a limited number of such people available. A prudently constructed constitutional system, therefore, will not disincentivize their political participation. But this is precisely what the *New York Times* doctrine does. It necessarily diminishes the number of people who will be willing to serve in public life by making public figures bear a heightened risk to their reputations. We would certainly diminish the willingness of citizens to hold public office if they had to pay an additional tax for doing so. The same pernicious effect results from telling citizens that they must submit to defamation, without effective redress, if they choose to enter public life.

Diminishing the size of the pool of people willing to serve necessarily harms the public's ability to choose those who will govern. Worse, the *New York Times* standard must also diminish the quality of the pool of people willing to serve. If the price of admission to public life is submission to defamation, then those citizens who are most solicitous of reputation, who care most about what their fellow citizens think of them, will be most deterred from public service. But those who are protective of their reputation are often the people of highest integrity. In any case, it is a poor policy that deters the honorable but not the shameless from entering public life.

The *New York Times* libel standard also erodes the quality of democratic deliberation. In a representative democracy, the people are to set the basic direction of public policy by electing public officials with whom they agree on the major issues confronting the country and whom they can trust to conduct their offices with ability and integrity. To perform this task well, the public needs accurate information about the candidates for public office. In a healthy democracy, the press would strive conscientiously to provide such information. It will, however, always be in the narrow interest of partisans—including a partisan press—to influence the outcomes of elections by misrepresenting the positions of candidates on controversial issues and by rendering the character of some candidates odious through defamation.

This, for example, is what the Hillary Clinton campaign and its supporters in the media intended to achieve by propagating the claim that Donald Trump was "colluding" with Russia. They thought that, in the absence of that false claim, Trump's platform might prove to be attractive to enough voters for him to win. Similarly, the enemies of Trump's presidency sought to politically marginalize him, to destroy his reputation, and to prevent his reelection by assailing him as a racist, including by propagating the demonstrably false claim that he had said that some neo-Nazis were "fine people."[14] Again, these false and defamatory claims were made so vigorously precisely because the people making them feared that, without them, Trump's actual priorities and actions as president might prove attractive to a majority of Americans.

New York Times v. Sullivan in fact encourages such behavior. The result is to diminish the quality of democratic government and even to reduce it to a sham. The quality is reduced because if the voters are not choosing candidates based on accurate information they might as well be choosing at random. More gravely, however, this situation tends to reduce our self-government to a sham because it deprives the voters of the opportunity to cast their ballots on the basis of genuine, informed consent. The political promise of the American regime is government by consent. Consent, however, can be denied not only by force but also by fraud. Where voters are manipulated into rejecting a candidate by political attacks resting on falsehoods, democracy itself has been in some measure defeated.

American democracy is committed not only to popular self-government but also to equality of rights. *New York Times v. Sullivan*, however, sets up an inequality of rights among different classes of citizens. Ordinary Americans enjoy the full protection of the law's traditional libel standards. In contrast, public figures—an expansive category that includes not only public officials and political candidates but also celebrities and practically anyone who has achieved any public prominence—are burdened with the "actual malice" standard, and accordingly have diminished reputational rights. But it is no more consistent with American principles to hold that the reputations of the famous should receive less protection than those of ordinary people than it would be to hold that the property of the rich should receive less protection than that of the middle class or the poor. The proper aim of the law is equally to protect the rights of all. Under such a principle, it makes no sense to hold that those who have succeeded in life—in many cases through their own efforts—should have to endure a higher risk of damage to reputation or to property. No sensibly governed democracy would tolerate such an arrangement.

Furthermore, the *New York Times* standard effectively makes journalism a privileged profession. Unlike all other professionals, journalists carry practically no liability for their negligence. If a physician carelessly prescribes an improper treatment and thus injures the health of a patient, he can be sued for his negligence. It will not be necessary to prove that he prescribed the treatment knowing it was wrong, or that he acted with reckless indifference to its harmfulness. Similarly, if a contractor carelessly damages a client's property, the client can recover damages because of the contractor's negligence—again, without having to show that the contractor acted with knowledge of the damage he would cause or reckless indifference to it. It is a violation of the principle of equality that all Americans are answerable for their negligence except for journalists. There is no reason to tolerate this inequality, especially when the deceptive reporting of journalists is so often damaging to the nation as a whole, while the damage caused by the negligence of other professionals is usually limited to unfortunate individuals.

Finally, the *New York Times* standard creates an unacceptable inequality between the media and ordinary citizens. Most national "reporting" in America is done not by independent journalists but by the employees of massive media corporations. These corporations make large sums of money by conveying information or alleged information. Thanks to our current libel standards, such corporations can make money by selling defamatory falsehoods about Americans, all the while being free from any real danger of having to pay damages to those whose right to reputation they have assailed for profit. Here it is especially helpful to recall that the kind of "public figure" to whom the *New York Times* standard applies may include any public official—a category that includes small town mayors and school board members, as well as anyone seeking such offices. The power of such people is negligible when compared to that of the corporations that might choose to make profitable "news" out of their lives, truthfully or not. Indeed, even most members of Congress have nothing like the megaphone possessed by the large corporations who report on their careers. The consequences of *New York Times v. Sullivan* thus savor more of oligarchy than democracy.

There is another way in which contemporary Americans tend to be blind to the damage caused by the "actual malice" standard. We are inclined to think that the *New York Times* ruling strikes a prudent balance between the key competing claims. After all, it seems reasonable to sacrifice the reputational interests of public figures the better to protect the right to freedom of the press. Such thinking, however, obscures the real nature of the costs imposed by the *New York Times* doctrine. Libel is not just an imposition on someone else's interests but an attack on the rights of another person—specifically, on the right to one's reputation.

This is the understanding that informed the principle of freedom of the press embodied in the First Amendment. This understanding was shaped in the first instance by the English tradition of common law, a tradition famously summarized by William Blackstone in his celebrated and influential *Commentaries on the Laws of England*. According to Blackstone, the "security of his reputation or good name from the arts of detraction and slander, are rights to which every man is entitled by reason and natural justice; since, without these, it is impossible to have the perfect enjoyment of any other advantage or right."[15]

It is worth emphasizing here that Blackstone presents security of reputation not only as a customary but a natural right. This view persisted in the political and legal culture of the Founding generation. Thus, for example, James Kent, in his *Commentaries on American Law*, treated libel in his lecture on "the Absolute Rights of Persons," and observed that "the preservation of every person's good name from the vile arts of detraction is justly included" as "a part of the right of personal security."[16] Similarly, James Wilson, in his *Lectures on Law*, referred to libel as "a crime against the right of reputation." He then went on to class libel with theft—a violation of the natural right to property—in its gravity: "robbery itself does not flow from a fountain more rankly poisoned, than that which throws out the waters of calumny and defamation."[17]

Justice Joseph Story, writing as a circuit judge in a federal district court in the case *Dexter v. Spear* (1825), likewise presented security of reputation as a right equally important as other rights commonly understood to be natural and fundamental by the Founders:

> The case of libels stands upon the same general grounds as other rights of action for wrongs. The general rule of law is, that whoever does an injury to another is liable in damages to the extent of that injury. It matters not, whether the injury is to the property, or the person, or the rights, or the reputation, of another. The law has declared all these entitled to its protection; and whoever wantonly assails them must answer in damages for the consequences. Civil society could not exist upon any other terms. Injuries to the reputation, by gross slanders and degrading libels, are oftentimes more extensive in mischief, and more fatal to the public peace and to private happiness, than any which can affect mere corporeal property. Indeed, the dearest property, which a man has, is often his good name and character.[18]

It is evident that the Founders' understanding is correct: security of reputation deserves to be classed as a natural right. This right is as deeply rooted in human nature as the right to personal safety or the right to security in one's property. Human beings are by nature sociable animals. They are made to live together not only in families but in a larger society. Accordingly, they have natural feelings of concern for what others think of them. Anyone with experience of human life knows that to be publicly defamed is just as unpleasant and harmful as to be robbed or assaulted—and often more so. Because human beings are naturally sociable, they require each other's help to exercise their rights fruitfully. Damage to reputation therefore harms one's ability to enjoy other rights. If the community believes that you are guilty of some vile transgression, it will be hard to have friends, hard to get married, hard to earn a living, and perhaps even hard to remain safe.

This account of reputation as a natural and fundamental right in turn informed the Founders' understanding of the scope of the freedom of the press. According to that understanding, libelous or defamatory publication is outside the freedom of the press, properly understood, and therefore is simply not protected by the First Amendment. This understanding was held, moreover, as applying across the board to all cases, without reference to any distinction between public figures and ordinary citizens. The heightened, "actual malice" standard that the *New York Times* Court imposed was accordingly a judicial invention not rooted in the original meaning of the First Amendment.[19]

The Founding-era idea of freedom of the press did not originate with the First Amendment. Americans of that period considered this freedom to be part of the inheritance of English liberty, which Blackstone had affirmed in his *Commentaries on the Laws of England*. Blackstone and the Americans of the Founding generation, however, also appreciated what contemporary Americans have often forgotten: that the "liberty" of the press must be distinguished from its "licentiousness." Libel belonged in the latter category—outside the scope of the proper liberty of the press—and was accordingly subject to legal punishment. According to Blackstone, the "liberty of the press, properly understood, is by no means infringed or violated" where "libels are punished under English law."[20]

American legal theory and practice at the time of the Founding did not perfectly mirror Blackstone's views and were more liberal in some respects.[21] Nevertheless, the Founding generation held to Blackstone's fundamental point that libel or defamation is not part of the liberty of the press. For example, James Kent's *Commentaries on American Law* affirmed that "the liberty of speech, and of the press, should be duly preserved" because the "liberal communication of sentiment, and entire freedom of discussion, in respect to the character and conduct of public men, and candidates for public favor, is deemed essential to the judicious exercise of the right of suffrage, and of that control over their rulers, which resides in the free people of these United States." At the same time, however, Kent also acknowledged the traditional view that a libel is a legal "grievance" and that "the law has accordingly considered it in the light of a public as well as a private injury."[22] Similarly, James Wilson's *Lectures on Law* observed that the "citizen under a free government has a right to think, to speak, to write, to print, and to publish freely, *but with decency and truth*, concerning public men, public bodies, and public measures."[23]

Justice Joseph Story gave a similar account of the relevant principles in the aforementioned *Dexter v. Spear*. There he explained that "no man has a right to state of another that which is false and injurious to him," and that consequently "no man has a right to give it wider and more mischievous range by publishing it in a newspaper." "The liberty of speech, or of the press," he continued, "has nothing to do with this subject"—namely, libel. These liberties "are not endangered by the punishment of libelous publications. The liberty of speech and the liberty of the press do not authorize malicious and injurious defamation. There can be no right in printers, any more than in other persons, to do wrong."[24]

As these passages indicate, the Founders understood that truthful criticism of public figures is a necessary component of republican self-government. They equally indicate, however, that the Founders placed false and defamatory claims in an entirely different category. Such claims, they held, make no positive contribution to self-government, are a violation of the right to reputation, and are accordingly not protected by freedom of the press.

Viewing the question superficially, it may seem that *New York Times v. Sullivan* adheres to the original meaning of the First Amendment by holding that a defamed person, including a public figure, may sue for libel and collect damages. But this is incorrect. The doctrine *of New York Times v. Sullivan* retains the shell of the traditional principle that libel is not protected by the First Amendment, but then makes it practically impossible for a public figure to sue for libel successfully—even when that public figure has in fact been the object of false and defamatory publication—by imposing the "actual malice" standard.

Justice Brennan's opinion in the *New York Times* case incorporates distinctions and standards into American libel law that are alien to the original meaning of the First Amendment.[25] Neither Blackstone, Kent, Wilson, nor Story suggest that some libel cases are to be adjudicated under separate standards that make it especially difficult for public figures to prevail. They say nothing of "actual malice" in the sense that the *New York Times* Court uses the term, but instead hold that a publication is libelous and actionable if it meets the simple test of being defamatory and false.[26]

CONCLUSION: SECURING LIBERTY WHILE PREVENTING LICENSE

The "actual malice" standard of *New York Times v. Sullivan* is bad in theory and bad in practice. It is inconsistent with the original meaning of the First Amendment, and it undermines key American principles such as individual rights, equality, and democratic self-government. This doctrine should be repudiated by the Supreme Court at the earliest opportunity.

Nevertheless, there is a danger in doing so. The danger arises from the increasingly illiberal character of the American Left. The Left has considerable institutional power, and it has revealed itself as more and more willing to suppress speech with which it disagrees. A common slogan of the Left holds that "hate speech is not free speech"—with the tacit understanding that "hate speech" often includes speech that asks questions that the Left would rather not have to answer. If the *New York Times* doctrine is rejected by the Court, it is not hard to imagine some on the Left seizing on the opportunity to contend that what they label as "hate speech" should be treated as actionable defamation. In order to avert this danger, it is necessary to clarify two crucial distinctions: between opinion and fact, in the first place, and between individual rights and group identity, in the second place.

The traditional understanding of libel—that which prevailed at the time of the Founding and for many generations afterward—always included the privilege of freely sharing one's opinions on public questions. As Blackstone observed, "Every freeman has an undoubted right to lay what sentiments he pleases before the public: to forbid this, is to destroy the freedom of the press."[27] Accordingly, even with effective standards against libel, citizens and media organizations will have considerable liberty to share whatever opinions they like about politicians, parties, and proposals. They may denounce their political opponents as fools, may inquire into and critique their motives, may label whole political parties as crazy or corrupt. What they cannot do, however, is use false facts to defame their opponents. Traditional libel standards do not even require participants to stick to the facts when they are engaged in political debate. They may opine with as much freedom and as much passion as they can muster. These standards only require them not to resort to defamatory falsehood. Such standards surely preserve the possibility of vigorous public debate while still averting the dangers of uncontrolled defamation.

Any reconsideration of *New York Times v. Sullivan* must also bear in mind that the core purpose of libel laws is to protect the individual right to reputation. On this view, while individuals can be injured by defamation and must have an effective right to seek justice, the same is not true of social groups. Nor may individuals seek damages because of alleged defamation of the group to which they belong. We live in an age in which group identity is celebrated and in which, accordingly, many people feel a sense of grievance if the group to which they belong is criticized. We should of course strive to maintain a due civility, but the purpose of libel laws is not to shield people's feelings from being hurt on the basis of the negative opinions that often accompany group differences but to protect the individual's right to his own reputation. Even with a restoration of traditional libel standards, the First Amendment will still offer a robust protection for freedom of debate, including the long-standing protection for ideas and utterances that many will find uncivil and even offensive.

Restoration of the pre-*New York Times v. Sullivan* libel standards will, however, establish a wholesome discipline for the American media. If the media attempt to make money and to influence politics by retailing false and defamatory materials about American citizens, they will have to contemplate the very real possibility of successful libel lawsuits. Reporters and editors will also have to consider the possibility that they might lose their jobs by getting their employer sued, along with the danger of the reputational damage to the media institution that will accompany a libel suit. And the CEOs of big media corporations will have to consider the financial harm that comes from paying out damages to litigants who successfully sue for libel. None of this would do anything to "chill" the robust exchange of information and ideas. To avoid these dangers, media institutions would need to do no more than make sure of the truth of what they publish, especially when the matter damages a person's reputation. There is nothing to lose and much to gain by insisting on such discipline—a discipline that would restore the original meaning of the First Amendment and would enhance rather than undermine our country's commitment to rights, equality, and democracy.

ABOUT THE AUTHOR

Carson Holloway is Ralph Wardle Diamond Professor of Arts and Sciences and professor of political science at the University of Nebraska, Omaha and a Washington Fellow in the Claremont Institute's Center for the American Way of Life. He is coeditor, with Bradford P. Wilson, of the two-volume work, *The Political Writings of Alexander Hamilton* (Cambridge University Press, 2017). He is also the author of *Hamilton versus Jefferson in the Washington Administration: Completing the Founding or Betraying the Founding?* (Cambridge University Press, 2015).

ACKNOWLEDGEMENTS

I wish to thank Jordan Cash, Matthew Franck, Arthur Milikh, Edward Morse, David Oakley, Douglas Walker, and Bradford Wilson for their helpful comments on earlier versions of this paper. I also wish to thank Paul Moreno for pointing me to some excellent sources. Finally, I owe thanks to Claremont interns Jack Little and Avery Bower for their research assistance.

ENDNOTES

1. See David A. Logan, "Rescuing Our Democracy by Rethinking *New York Times Co. v. Sullivan*," *Ohio State Law Journal* 81 (2020): 759.

2. Justice Clarence Thomas, concurring opinion in *Kathrine Mae McKee v. William H. Cosby, Jr.* (2019), 586 U. S. _____ (2019).

3. *New York Times Co. v. Sullivan*, 376 U.S. 254 (1964), at 254.

4. *Gertz v. Robert Welch, Inc.*, 418 U.S. 323 (1974), at 323.

5. Logan, "Rescuing Our Democracy by Rethinking *New York Times Co. v. Sullivan*," 778.

6. Logan, "Rescuing Our Democracy by *Rethinking New York Times Co. v. Sullivan*," 809.

7. Alfred H. Kelly, "Constitutional Liberty and the Law of Libel: A Historians View," *American Historical Review* 74 (December 1968): 439.

8. Ibid., 439–40.

9. See *O'Donnell v. Philadelphia Record Company* (1947), https://casetext.com/case/odonnell-v-phila-record-co.

10. See William L. Dwyer, *The Goldmark Case: An American Libel Trial* (Seattle: University of Washington Press, 1984).

11. Peter Gorner, "*Time* vs. Sharon: A Question of Intent," *Chicago Tribune*, April 15, 1987, https://www.chicagotribune.com/news/ct-xpm-1987-04-15-8701280653-story.html.

12. Noelle Swan, "George Zimmerman Loses Defamation Case Against NBC: Why?" *Christian Science Monitor*, June 30, 2014, https://www.csmonitor.com/USA/USA-Update/2014/0630/George-Zimmerman-loses-defamation-suit-against-NBC.-Why.

13. Jeremy W. Peters, "Sarah Palin's Libel Claim Against the *Times* is Rejected by a Jury," *New York Times*, February 15, 2022, https://www.nytimes.com/2022/02/15/business/media/new-york-times.html.

14. President Trump had in fact said that there were "fine people" on both sides in the Charlottesville protest of 2017, while going on a moment later to add: "and I'm not talking about the neo-Nazis and the white nationalists, because they should be condemned totally." See "Full Text: Trump's Comments on White Supremacists, Alt-Left in Charlottesville," *Politico*, August 15, 2007, https://www.politico.com/story/2017/08/15/full-text-trump-comments-white-supremacists-alt-left-transcript-241662.

15. William Blackstone, *Commentaries on the Laws of England*, a facsimile of the first edition of 1765–1769, ed. Thomas A. Green, vol. 1 (Chicago: University of Chicago Press, 1979), 130.

16. James Kent, *Commentaries on American Law*, vol. 2 (New York: O. Halsted, 1827), 12.

17. James Wilson, "Lectures on Law," in *Collected Works of James Wilson*, ed. Kermit L. Hall and Mark David Hall, vol. 2 (Carmel, IN: Liberty Fund, 2007), 1136.

18. *Dexter v. Spear*, 7 F. Cas. 624 (No. 3,867), Circuit Court of Rhode Island (1825).

19. As James Stoner observes, Brennan and his colleagues did not pull the actual malice standard out of "thin air." Rather, they found it in use as a "common-law rule developed in several jurisdictions" and decided to adopt it as a "national standard." See Stoner's *Common-Law Liberty: Rethinking American Constitutionalism* (Lawrence: University Press of Kansas, 2003), 44. Nevertheless, the development of such a standard by some state courts did not and could not turn the rule into a requirement of the First Amendment. Accordingly, *New York Times v. Sullivan* remains an act of unconstitutional judicial activism—even if the justices did not themselves invent the actual malice standard in the course of deciding the case.

20. Blackstone, *Commentaries on the Laws of England*, vol. 1, at 150–52.

21. Blackstone, for example, held that the truth of a defamatory statement was not a defense against a criminal libel. This view

would probably have been controversial to Founding-era Americans and was in any case discarded by the early nineteenth century. Moreover, it is doubtful that the more democratic Americans would have agreed with the rather aristocratic English view expressed by Blackstone that libel is especially bad when directed against a magistrate.

22.   James Kent, *Commentaries on American Law*, 13–14.

23.   James Wilson, "Lectures on Law," in *Collected Works of James Wilson*, 1046. Emphasis added.

24.   *Dexter v. Spear*, 7 F. Cas. 624 (No. 3,867), Circuit Court of Rhode Island (1825). For Story's similar account of the original meaning of the First Amendment itself, see his *Commentaries on the Constitution of the United States*, vol. 3 (Boston: Hilliard, Gray, 1833), 731–33.

25.   Although the standards devised in *New York Times v. Sullivan* are not rooted in the original meaning of the First Amendment, the Court tried to create an illusion of originalist legitimacy for its decision by invoking the Founding-era debate over the Sedition Act. That act was condemned by many prominent Americans despite the fact that it explicitly acknowledged truth as a defense against a charge of seditious libel. On this basis, Brennan claimed that the Sedition Act had been found constitutionally invalid "in the court of history"—and he thus sought support in the Founding for his claim that even factually erroneous and defamatory publications are protected by the First Amendment. Brennan's account here is, to say the least, tendentious. It is of course true that the Sedition Act was condemned as unconstitutional by weighty figures such as Thomas Jefferson and James Madison. It is also true, however, that it was held to be constitutional by figures of no less consequence and legal sagacity, such as Alexander Hamilton and John Adams. One congress, in 1840, declared the Act to be unconstitutional; but another, in 1798, had affirmed its constitutionality by enacting it in the first place. President Jefferson acted officially on his belief in the act's unconstitutionality; but President Adams had expressed his official approval of it by signing it into law in the first place. No impartial judge could draw from these conflicting opinions a firm conclusion that the Sedition Act had been found unconstitutional "in the court of history."

26. Some of these commentators say that "malice" is necessary to a libel. This is not a reference to the modern "actual malice" standard, however. Traditionally, malice was assumed as a matter of law when the publication itself was libelous. See Herman Belz, Winfred Harbison, and Alfred H. Kelly, *The American Constitution: Its Origins and Development*, 7th ed., vol. 2 (New York: WW Norton, 1991), 624.

27. Blackstone, *Commentaries*, vol. 4, 150.

www.ingramcontent.com/pod-product-compliance
Lightning Source LLC
Chambersburg PA
CBHW051406250726